Let's Draw!

This edition published by Parragon Books Ltd in 2016

Parragon Books Ltd
Chartist House
15–17 Trim Street
Bath BA1 1HA, UK
www.parragon.com

Written by Frances Prior-Reeves
Designed by Talking Design
Illustrations by Carol Seatory

ISBN 978-1-4748-5031-5
Printed in China

Let's Draw!

PaRragon

Bath · New York · Cologne · Melbourne · Delhi
Hong Kong · Shenzhen · Singapore

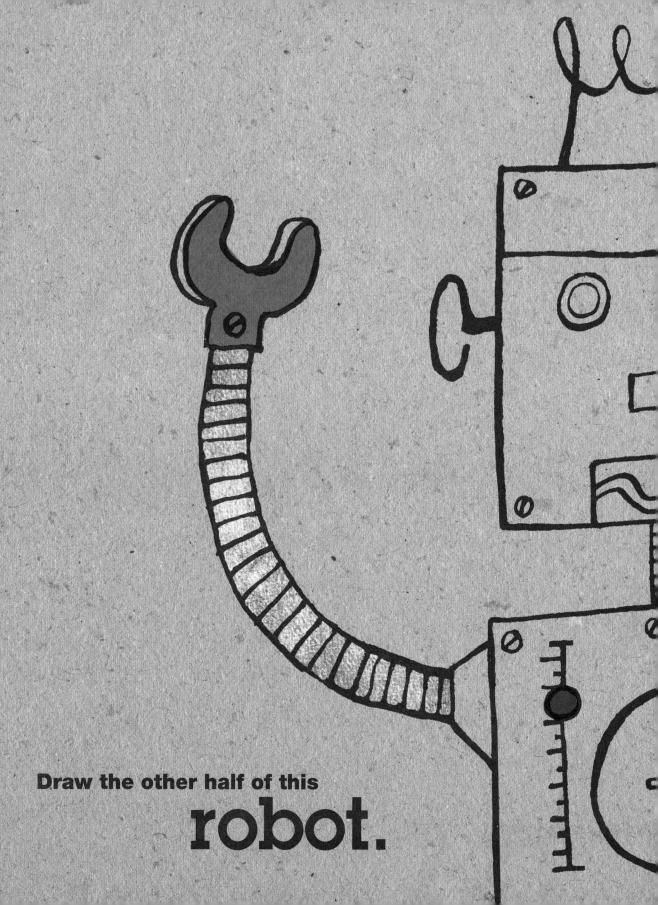

Draw the other half of this
robot.

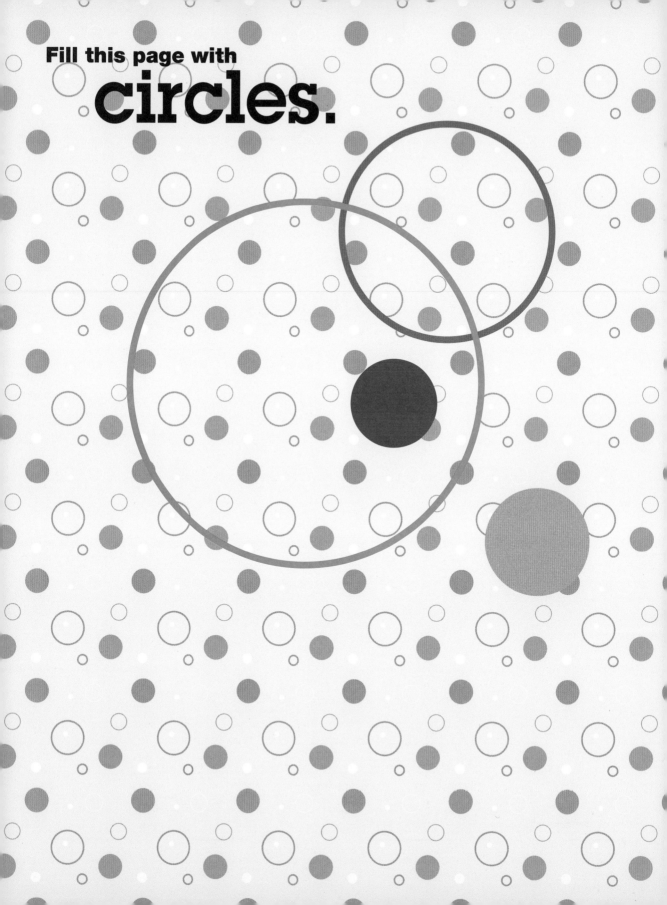

Fill this page with
circles.

Can you turn those circles into faces?

Draw your favourite
mythical creature.

Colour in this classic pattern to give it a more **contemporary feel.**

Your creative space.

Add your own design to this

vase.

Design a pot in any shape and then add your own detail.

Fill these **shelves.**

Fill these pages with bright and colourful monsters to play with.

Fill this page with

squares.

Can you turn those squares into
robots and
machines?

Fill these pages with beautiful
butterflies.

Draw half of **your** face on one side of the circle and draw half of a **monkey's** face on the other side.

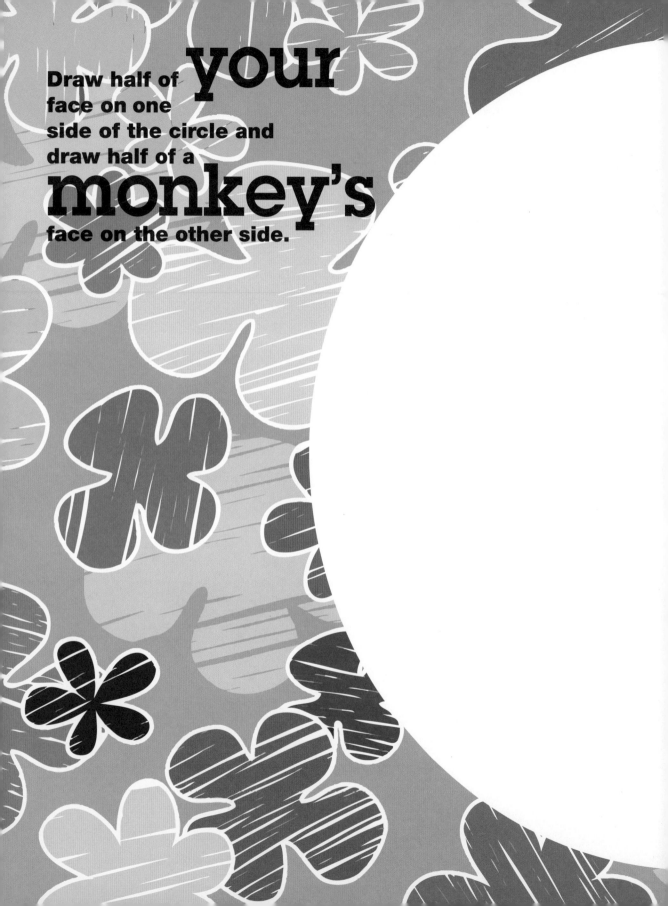

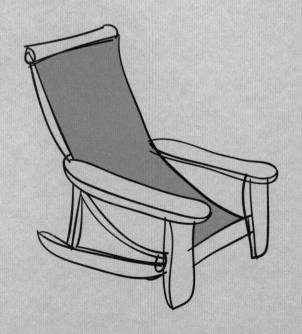

Draw, shade, doodle and colour anything.

Add colour, texture and patterns to this spiral.

**Draw the other
half of this
train.**

Design these fabulous **tiles** so that each one is unique.

Draw a rocket

flying to the moon.

Use the gridlines to guide your doodles.

Fill this room with furniture.

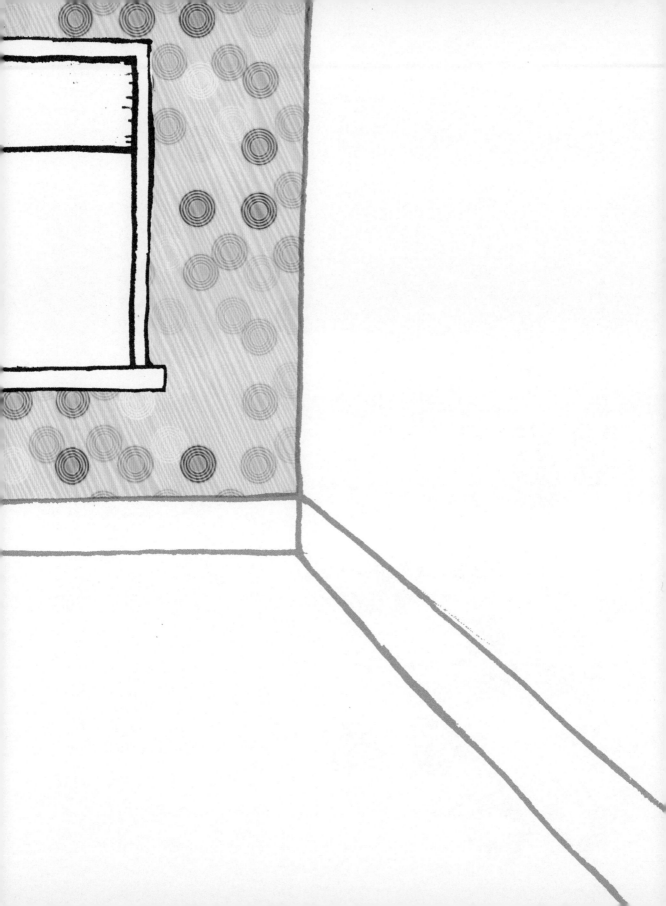

Fill these pages with different
animal footprints.

Fill this **seabed** with life.

Fill these jars with your favourite
sweets and biscuits.

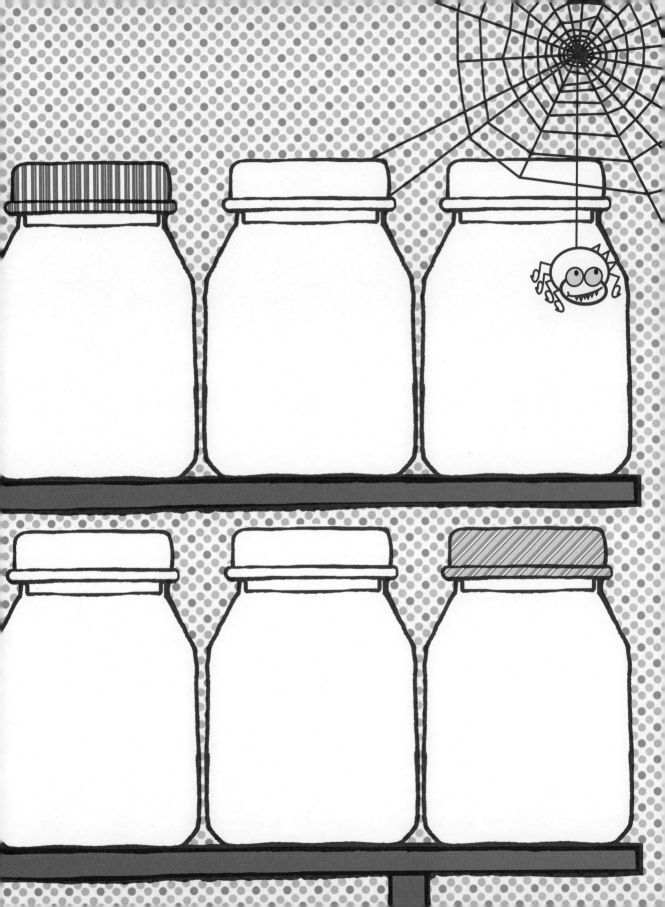

Draw our galaxy;
the milky way.

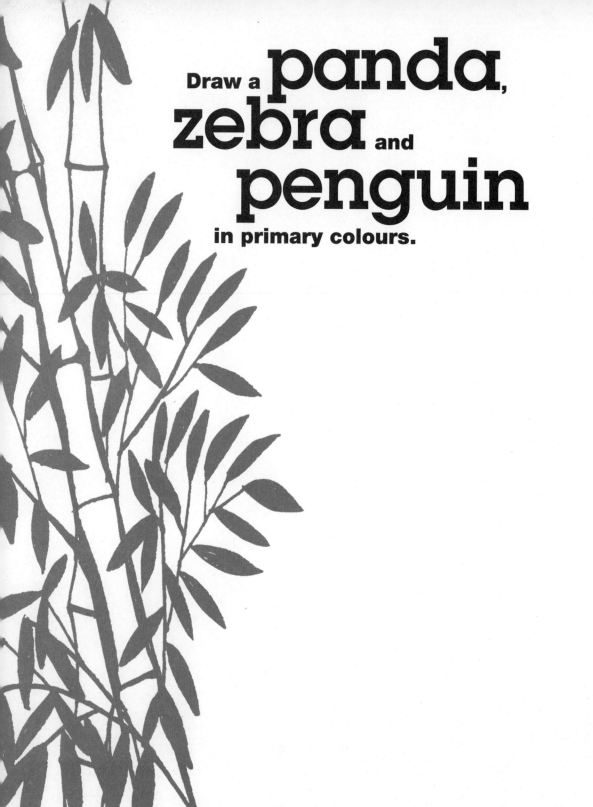

Draw a **panda**, **zebra** and **penguin** in primary colours.

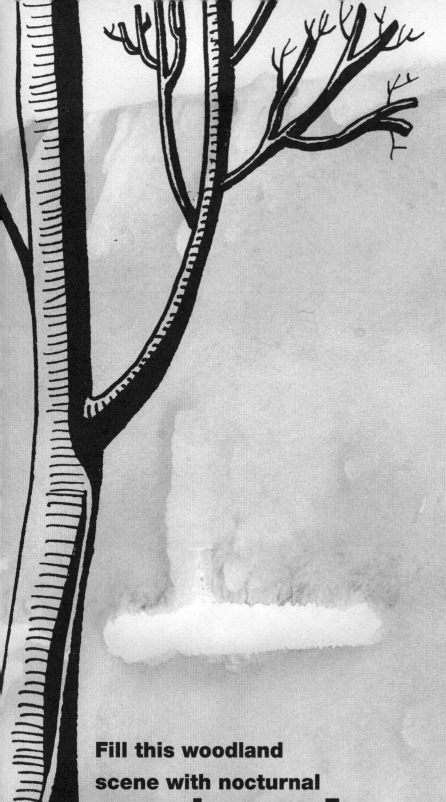

**Fill this woodland
scene with nocturnal
animals.**

Fill this page with diamonds.

Can you turn those diamonds into something alive?

Plant a **flower garden** on these pages.

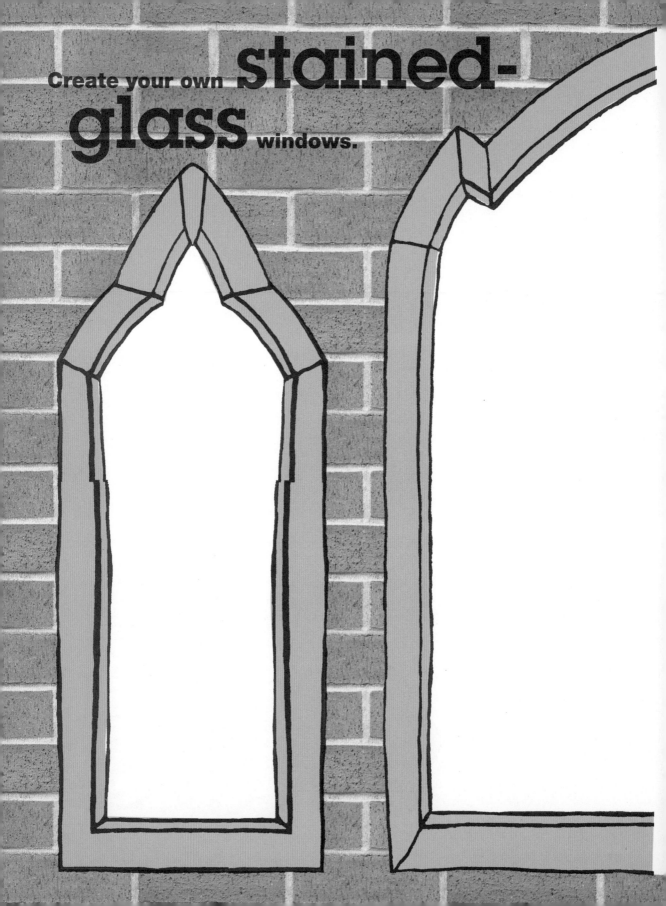

Create your own **stained-glass** windows.

Finish this cityscape.

Draw some cars on this road.

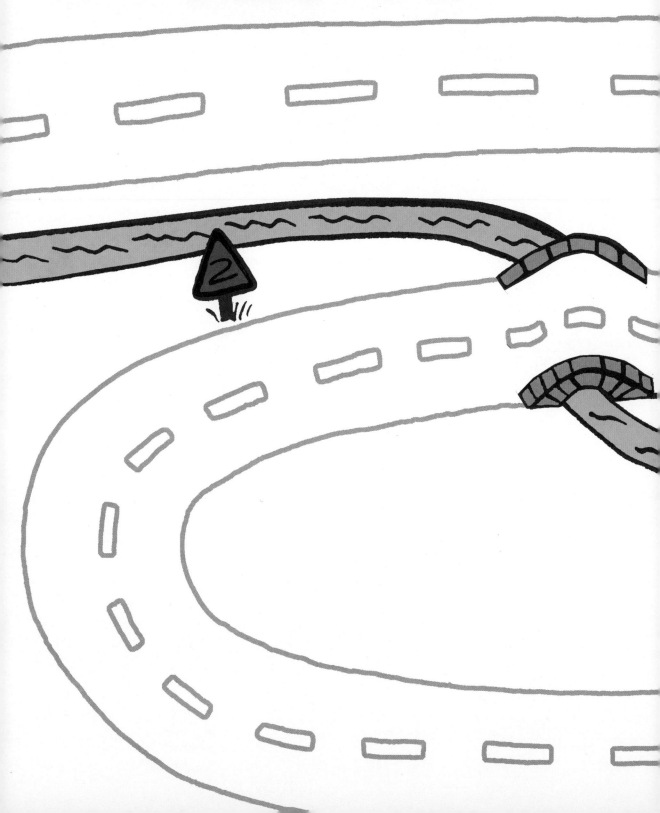

Finish the design on this rug.

Add personalities to the
people <small>in this crowd.</small>

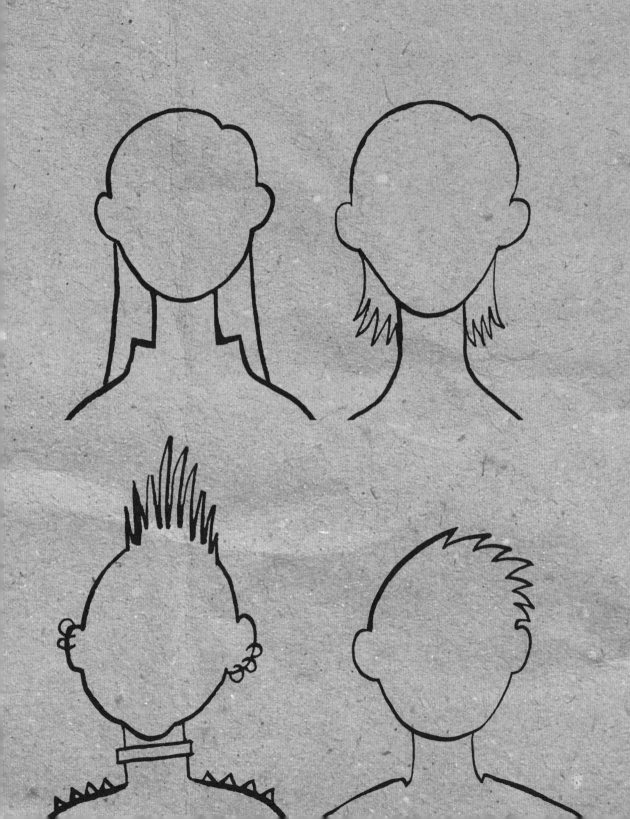

Fill this jar with

jelly beans.

Fill this page with stars.

**Can you change those
stars into patterns?**

Fill the sky and trees with birds.

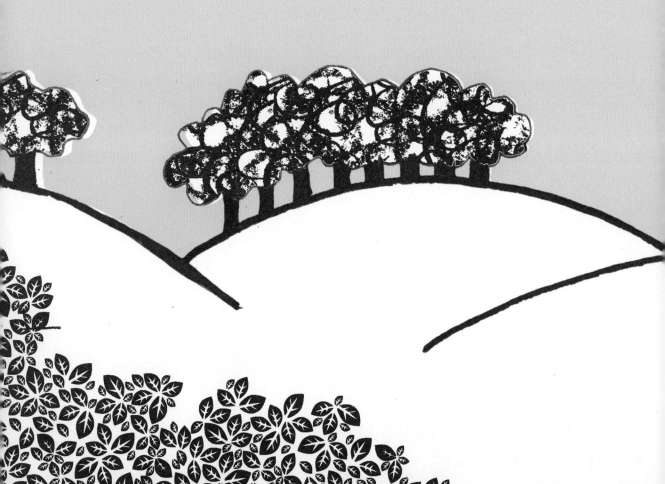

Colour these pages.

Colour these party hats.

Now design your own.

Create a
masterpiece
to go in this frame
above the mantelpiece.

Turn these shapes into **fish.**

Colour every other square.

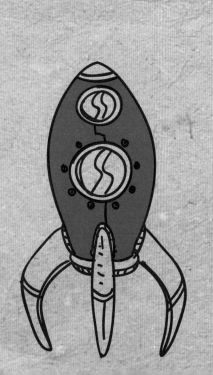

Design a beautiful
ball gown
for this girl.

Design an accompanying outfit for this boy.

Doodle **cats** and **dogs.**

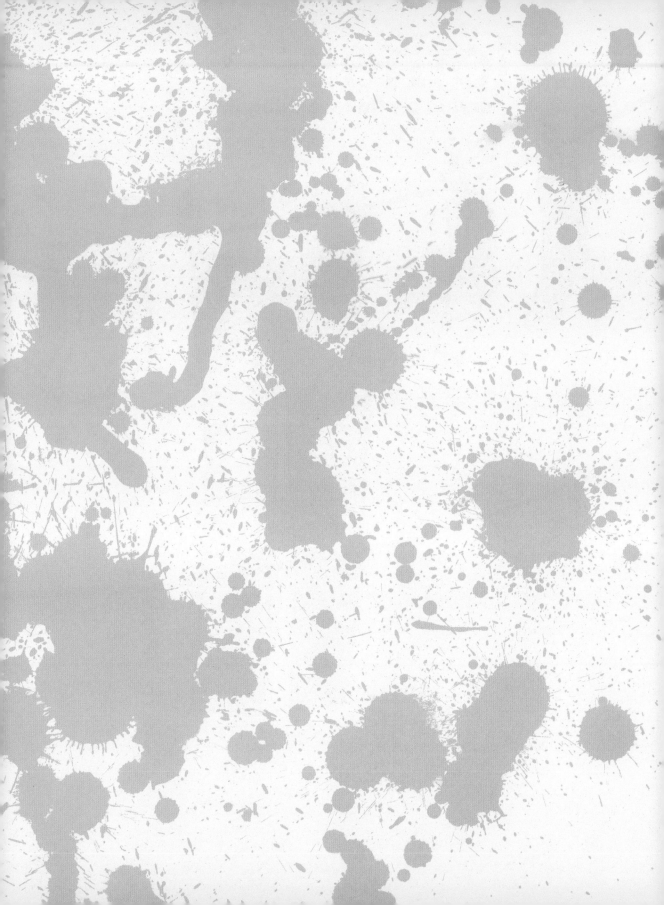

Draw clothes
drying on this washing line.

Draw what's above and below the
sea level.

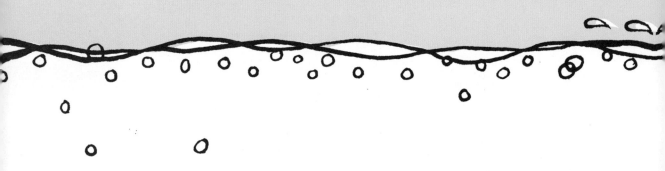

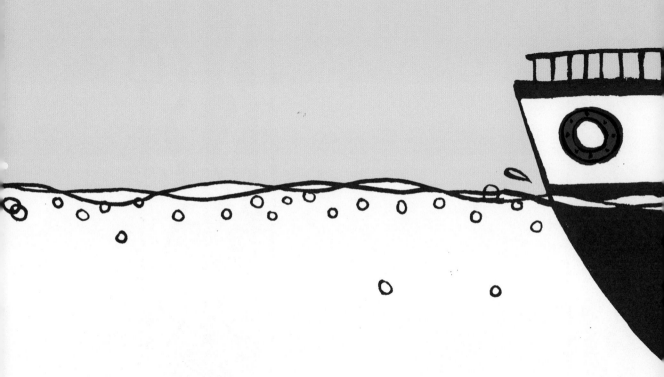

Fill these frames with
abstract art.

Drawing is
creating!

Fill this jar with
coins.

Draw this princess
a tower.

Fill these pages with

snowflakes.

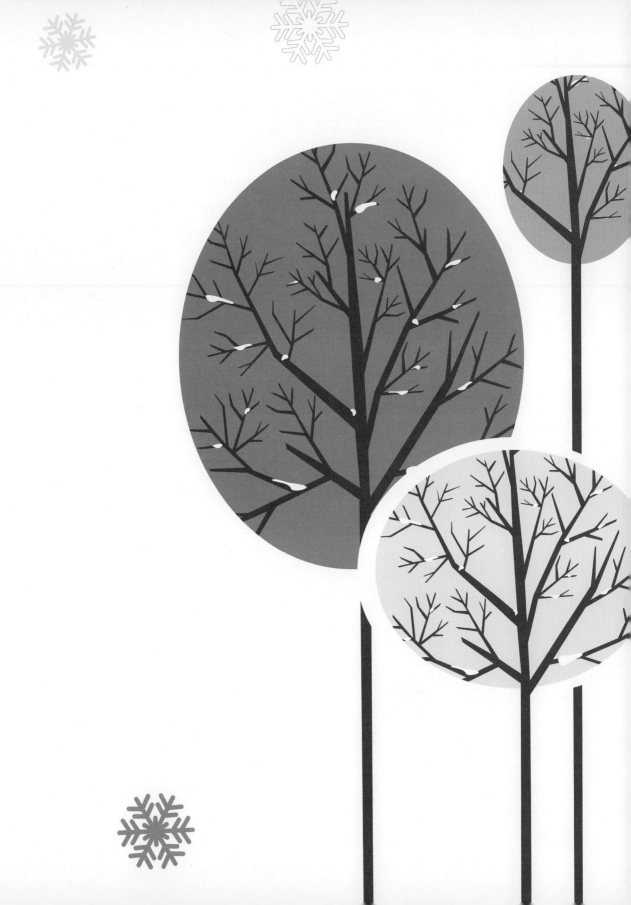

Fill these pages with
fairies.

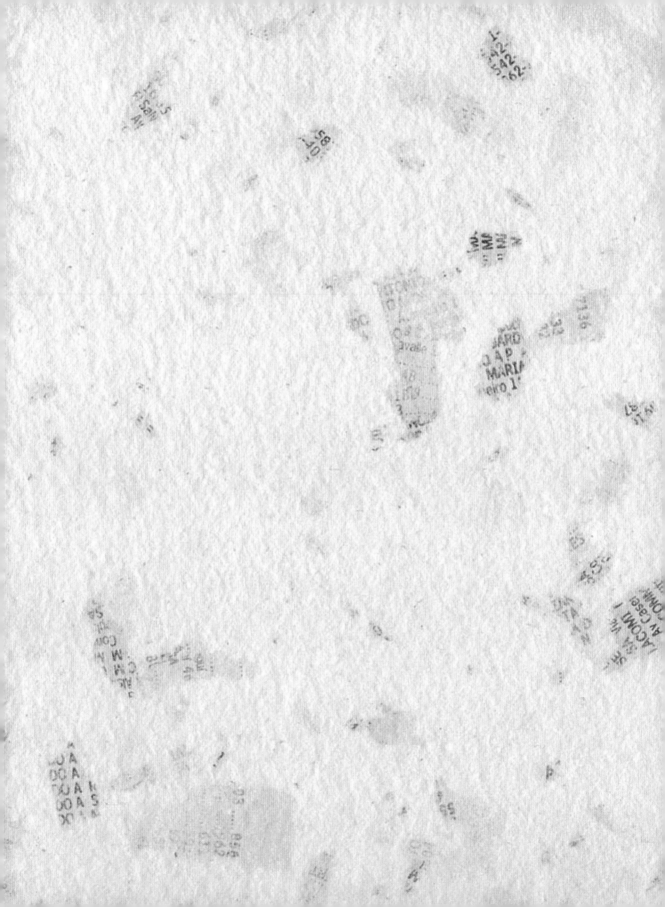

Fill these pages with

patterned hearts.

Add life to this
planet.

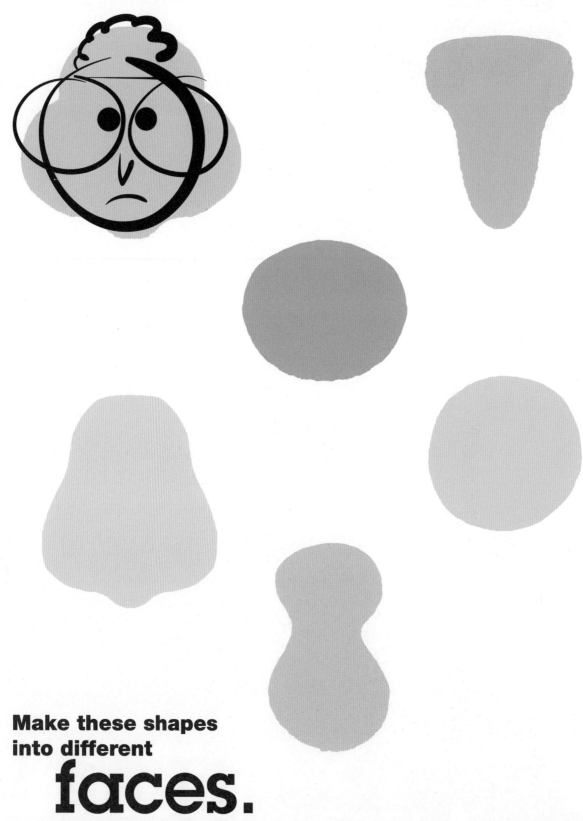

**Make these shapes
into different
faces.**

Draw the ingredients
for your favourite meal.

Fill this plate with your favourite food.

Colour these shoes.

Now design your own.

Design these cushions.

Draw the other half of this
teddy bear.

Add more vehicles to create a
traffic jam.

Design the hot-air balloons in this race.

Draw a garden

that can be seen through these patio doors.

Doodle **frogs** and **flies.**

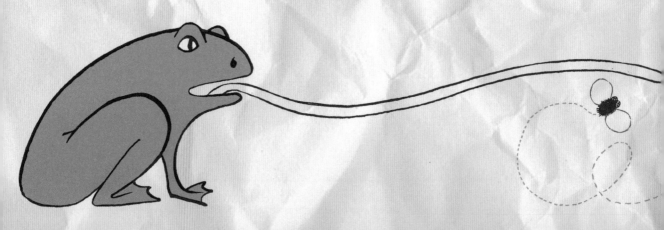

Give these flowers **petals.**